ALL
minus one

INTRODUCTION

From street battles over controversial speakers in Berkeley, California to the "no platforming" movement in British universities to the expansion of hate crime laws in Canada, the English speaking countries are consumed by debates over free speech. The conflict is fiercest on university campuses. Both sides point to rights that must be protected; both sides point to harms that will be suffered if the other side gets its way. Neither side seems able to convince the other with logic, shame, or violence. It is time to step back and look at the big picture. Why is free speech important in a modern liberal democracy?

The liberal democratic case for free speech was set out in 1859 by John Stuart Mill, the English philosopher, politician, and activist, in his famous essay *On Liberty*. That was more than a century and half ago but his arguments have enduring value, especially for students and teachers (who, if they are any good, are students too). That is why we have decided to publish an edited extract of *On Liberty*. The text you are about to read is a little more than half of chapter 2 of Mill's book, or about a fifth of the entire work. Our goal was to make it easy and enjoyable for a new generation to discover Mill's best ideas on free speech with just an hour or so of reading.

About us: We are an odd bunch, to be honest: a Mill scholar who studies inequality at the Brookings Institution (Reeves), a social psychologist who studies morality at New York University's Stern School of Business (Haidt), and an illustrator who loves provocative ideas (Cicirelli). We were drawn together by chance encounters in which we discovered a shared belief that Mill deserves a wider audience, especially among people embarking on a college education. Since Mill's writing is unusually rich in metaphors and images, we wanted to convey some of his ideas visually, too.

More about Mill: John Stuart Mill (1806-1873) is one of the most important thinkers in the liberal tradition. He was also an activist. He campaigned for women's rights, and was the first MP to introduce a bill for women's suffrage into parliament. He was a fiercely committed anti-racist, strongly supporting the abolitionist movement in the U.S., and the North in the Civil War. Mill also led a successful campaign for the right to protest and speak in London's public parks. In Hyde Park, the famous Speaker's Corner stands today as a tribute to his victory.

Mill's main concern was not government censorship. It was the stultifying consequences of social conformity, of a culture where deviation from a prescribed set of opinions is punished through peer pressure and the fear of ostracism. "Protection, therefore, against the tyranny of the magistrate is not enough," he wrote. "There needs protection also against the tyranny of the prevailing opinion and feeling". Mill saw people even as brilliant as Charles Darwin living in fear of the response their views would provoke.

Mill was writing in Victorian England, but his fears are perhaps even more pressing today as we all struggle to adapt to a new technology and a new social order. Social media can now bring shame, angry mobs, and reputational destruction raining down on people within hours merely for expressing their honest opinions. Young people are particularly vulnerable to such pressures, given their heavy use of social media, and this is part of the reason why college campuses have become ground zero in the speech wars.
In the English speaking countries, uni-

versities are supposed to be special places where dissent is prized and new and even radical ideas can be tested. As judge Alex Kozinski wrote in 2010 in a major case regarding the First Amendment to the US Constitution:

The right to provoke, offend, and shock lies at the core of the First Amendment. This is particularly so on college campuses. Intellectual advancement has traditionally progressed through discord and dissent, as a diversity of views ensures that ideas survive because they are correct, not because they are popular.

Judge Kozinski was essentially channeling Mill, as you'll see. But what would Mill think of today's college campuses? What would he think about the growing number of students and professors who say that they are afraid to speak up, not because they fear the government but because they fear each other?

Mill's basic lesson was the timeless truth that we need each other—even our opponents—more than we realize. We all tend to be arrogant and overconfident that "our side" is right. We all suffer from the "confirmation bias"—the tendency to search only for evidence that will confirm our existing beliefs and prejudices. This is why diversity is so important, particularly diversity of viewpoints: The only reliable cure for the confirmation bias is interacting with other people who have a different confirmation bias, and who do you the favor of criticizing your ideas.

Mill believed that the pursuit of truth required the collation and combination of ideas and propositions, even those that seem to be in opposition to each other. He urged us to allow others to speak—and then to listen to them—for three main reasons.

First, the other person's idea, however controversial it seems today, might turn out to be right. ("The opinion may possibly be true.")

Second, even if our opinion is largely correct, we hold it more rationally and securely as a result of being challenged. ("He who knows only his own side of the case, knows little of that.")

Third, and in Mill's view most likely, opposing views may each contain a portion of the truth, which need to be combined. ("Conflicting doctrines share the truth between them.")

For free speech to be valuable to the pursuit of truth, we all need to be both humble and open. We need humility to recognize that we might not be right about everything all of the time, and that we have something to learn from others. We also need to be open to the possibility of altering our views, opinions, and even values based on our engagement with the world. In other words, our identity as a person must be kept separable from the ideas we happen to endorse at a given time. Otherwise, when those ideas are criticized, we are likely to experience a conversation, book, or lecture as an attack upon our self, rather than as an opportunity to think about something more deeply.

Humility, openness, engagement, a strong and maturing self that is always a work in progress; these are the necessary ingredients for a free society, and for shared progress, according to Mill (who changed his mind about many things during the course of his life).

That's enough from us. Time for the main event. Mill opens his argument for free speech by imagining a world in which just one person holds a view contrary to that held by the rest of humanity. What harm could be done by silencing this lone eccentric?

ALL
minus one

JOHN STUART MILL'S IDEAS ON
FREE SPEECH ILLUSTRATED

Edited by Richard V. Reeves
and Jonathan Haidt

Art & Design by Dave Cicirelli

All Minus One was produced by Heterodox Academy.

"THE OPINION MAY POSSIBLY BE TRUE"

If all mankind minus one, were of one opinion, and only one person were of the contrary opinion, mankind would be no more justified in silencing that one person, than he, if he had the power, would be justified in silencing mankind...

The peculiar evil of silencing the expression of an opinion is, that it is robbing the human race; posterity as well as the existing generation; those who dissent from the opinion, still more than those who hold it. If the opinion is right, they are deprived of the opportunity of exchanging error for truth: if wrong, they lose, what is almost as great a benefit, the clearer perception and livelier impression of truth, produced by its collision with error.

We can never be sure that the opinion we are endeavouring to stifle is a false opinion; and if we were sure, stifling it would be an evil still.

First: the opinion which it is attempted to suppress by authority may possibly be true. Those who desire to suppress it, of course deny its truth; but they are not infallible.

They have no authority to decide the question for all mankind, and exclude every other person from the means of judging. To refuse a hearing to an opinion, because they are sure that it is false, is to assume that their certainty is the same thing as absolute certainty. All silencing of discussion is an assumption of infallibility. Its condemnation may be allowed to rest on this common argument, not the worse for being common.

Unfortunately for the good sense of mankind, the fact of their fallibility is far from carrying the weight in their practical judgment, which is always allowed to it in theory; for while every one well knows himself to be fallible, few think it necessary to take any precautions against their own fallibility, or admit the supposition that any opinion, of which they feel very certain, may be one of the examples of the error to which they acknowledge themselves to be liable.

Absolute princes, or others who are accustomed to unlimited deference, usually feel this complete confidence in their own opinions on nearly all subjects. People more happily situated, who sometimes hear their opinions disputed, and are not wholly unused to be set right when they are wrong, place the same unbounded reliance only on such of their opinions as are shared by all who surround them, or to whom they habitually defer: for in proportion to a man's want of confidence in his own solitary judgment, does he usually repose, with implicit trust, on the infallibility of "the world" in general. And the world, to each individual, means the part of it with which he comes in contact; his party, his sect, his church, his class of society: the man may be called, by comparison, almost liberal and large-minded to whom it means anything so comprehensive as his own country or his own age.

Nor is his faith in this collective authority at all shaken by his being aware that other ages, countries, sects, churches, classes, and parties have thought, and even now think, the exact reverse. He devolves upon his own world the responsibility of being in the right against the dissentient [differing, dissenting] worlds of other people; and it never troubles him that mere accident has decided which of these numerous worlds is the object of his reliance, and that the same causes which make him a Churchman in London, would have made him a Buddhist or a Confucian in Pekin [Beijing]. Yet it is as evident in itself, as any amount of argument can make it, that ages are no more infallible than individuals; every age having held many opinions which subsequent ages have deemed not only false but absurd; and

it is as certain that many opinions, now general, will be rejected by future ages, as it is that many, once general, are rejected by the present.

The objection likely to be made to this argument, would probably take some such form as the following[:] There is no greater assumption of infallibility in forbidding the propagation of error, than in any other thing which is done by public authority on its own judgment and responsibility. Judgment is given to men that they may use it. Because it may be used erroneously, are men to be told that they ought not to use it at all? To prohibit what they think pernicious, is not claiming exemption from error, but fulfilling the duty incumbent on them, although fallible, of acting on their conscientious conviction... There is no such thing as absolute certainty, but there is assurance sufficient for the purposes of human life. We may, and must, assume our opinion to be true for the guidance of our own conduct: and it is assuming no more when we forbid bad men to pervert society by the propagation of opinions which we regard as false and pernicious.

I answer, that it is assuming very much more. There is the greatest difference between presuming an opinion to be true, because, with every opportunity for contesting it, it has not been refuted, and assuming its truth for the purpose of not permitting its refutation. Complete liberty of contradicting and disproving our opinion, is the very condition which justifies us in assuming its truth for purposes of action; and on no other terms can a being with human faculties have any rational assurance of being right.

When we consider either the history of opinion, or the ordinary conduct of human life, to what is it to be ascribed that the one and the other are no worse than they are? Not certainly to the inherent force of the human understanding; for, on any matter not self-evident, there are ninety-nine persons totally incapable of judging of it, for one who is capable; and the capacity of the hundredth person is only comparative: for the majority of the eminent men of every past generation held many opinions now known to be erroneous, and did or approved numerous things which no one will now justify. Why is it, then, that there is on the whole a preponderance among mankind of rational opinions and rational conduct? If there really is this preponderance—which there must be unless human affairs are, and have always been, in an almost desperate state—it is owing to a quality of the human mind, the source of everything respectable in man either as an intellectual or as a moral being, namely, that his errors are corrigible. He is capable of rectifying his mistakes, by discussion and experience. Not by experience alone. There must be discussion, to show how experience is to be interpreted.

Wrong opinions and practices gradually yield to fact and argument: but facts and arguments, to produce any effect on the mind, must be brought before it. Very few facts are able to tell their own story, without comments to bring out their meaning. The whole strength and value, then, of human judgment, depending on the one property, that it can be set right when it is wrong, reliance can be placed on it only when the means of setting it right are kept constantly at hand. In the case of any person whose judgment is really deserving of confidence, how has it become so? Because he has kept his mind open to criticism of his opinions and conduct. Because it has been his practice to listen to all that could be said against him; to profit by as much of it as was just, and expound to himself, and upon occasion to others, the fallacy of what was fallacious. Because he has felt, that the only way in which a human being can make some approach to knowing the whole of a subject, is by hearing what can be said about it by persons of every variety of opinion, and studying all modes in which it can be looked at by every character of mind. No wise man ever acquired his wisdom in any mode but this; nor is it in the nature of human intellect to become wise in any other manner.

The steady habit of correcting and completing his own opinion by collating it with those of others, so far from causing doubt and hesitation in carrying it into practice, is the only stable foundation for a just reliance on it: for, being cognisant of all that can, at least obviously, be said against him, and having taken up his position against all gainsayers—knowing that he has sought for objections and difficulties, instead of avoiding them, and has shut out no light which can be thrown upon the subject from any quarter—he has a right to think his judgment better than that of any person, or any multitude, who have not gone through a similar process.

It is not too much to require that what the wisest of mankind, those who are best entitled to trust their own judgment, find necessary to warrant their relying on it, should be submitted to by that miscellaneous collection of a few wise and many foolish individuals, called the public… The Roman Catholic Church, even at the canonization of a saint, admits, and listens patiently to, a "devil's advocate." The holiest of men, it appears, cannot be admitted to posthumous honours, until all that the devil could say against him is known and weighed…

Strange it is, that men should admit the validity of the arguments for free discussion, but object to their being "pushed to an extreme;" not seeing that unless the reasons are good for an extreme case, they are not good for any case. Strange that they should imagine that they are not assuming infallibility, when they acknowledge that there should be free discussion on all subjects which can possibly be doubtful, but think that some particular principle or doctrine should be forbidden to be questioned because it is certain, that is, because they are certain that it is certain. To call any proposition certain, while there is any one who would deny its certainty if permitted, but who is not permitted, is to assume that we ourselves, and those who agree with us, are the judges of certainty, and judges without hearing the other side.

In the present age—which has been described as "destitute of faith, but terrified at scepticism"—in which people feel sure, not so much that their opinions are true, as that they should not know what to do without them—the claims of an opinion to be protected from public attack are rested not so much on its truth, as on its importance to society. There are, it is alleged, certain beliefs, so useful, not to say indispensable to well-being, that it is as much the duty of governments to uphold those beliefs, as to protect any other of the interests of society. In a case of such necessity, and so directly in the line of their duty, something less than infallibility may, it is maintained, warrant, and even bind, governments, to act on their own opinion, confirmed by the general opinion of mankind. It is also often argued, and still oftener thought, that none but bad men would desire to weaken these salutary beliefs; and there can be nothing wrong, it is thought, in restraining bad men, and prohibiting what only such men would wish to practise.

This mode of thinking makes the justification of restraints on discussion not a question of the truth of doctrines, but of their usefulness; and flatters itself by that means to escape the responsibility of claiming to be an infallible judge of opinions. But those who thus satisfy themselves, do not perceive that the assumption of infallibility is merely shifted from one point to another. The usefulness of an opinion is itself matter of opinion: as disputable, as open to discussion, and requiring discussion as much, as the opinion itself...

[T]he dictum that truth always triumphs over persecution, is one of those pleasant falsehoods which men repeat after one another till they pass into commonplaces, but which all experience refutes.

HISTORY TEEMS WITH INSTANCES OF TRUTH PUT DOWN BY PERSECUTION. IF NOT SUPPRESSED FOR EVER, IT MAY BE THROWN BACK FOR CENTURIES.

To speak only of religious opinions: the Reformation broke out at least twenty times before Luther, and was put down… Protestantism was rooted out; and, most likely, would have been so in England, had Queen Mary lived, or Queen Elizabeth died. Persecution has always succeeded, save where the heretics were too strong a party to be effectually persecuted. No reasonable person can doubt that Christianity might have been extirpated in the Roman Empire. It spread, and became predominant, because the persecutions were only occasional, lasting but a short time, and separated by long intervals of almost undisturbed propagandism.

It is a piece of idle sentimentality that truth, merely as truth, has any inherent power denied to error, of prevailing against the dungeon and the stake. Men are not more zealous for truth than they often are for error, and a sufficient application of legal or even of social penalties will generally succeed in stopping the propagation of either. The real advantage which truth has, consists in this, that when an opinion is true, it may be extinguished once, twice, or many times, but in the course of ages there will generally be found persons to rediscover it, until some one of its reappearances falls on a time when from favourable circumstances it escapes persecution until it such head as to withstand all subsequent attempts to suppress it...

[O]pinion, on this subject, is as efficacious as law; men might as well be imprisoned, as excluded from the means of earning their bread. Those whose bread is already secured, and who desire no favours from men in power, or from bodies of men, or from the public, have nothing to fear from the open avowal of any opinions, but to be ill-thought of and ill-spoken of, and this it ought not to require a very heroic mould to enable them to bear. There is no room for

any appeal ad misericordiam [on grounds of pity] in behalf of such persons. But though we do not now inflict so much evil on those who think differently from us, as it was formerly our custom to do, it may be that we do ourselves as much evil as ever by our treatment of them. Socrates was put to death, but the Socratic philosophy rose like the sun in heaven, and spread its illumination over the whole intellectual firmament. Christians were cast to the lions, but the Christian church grew up a stately and spreading tree, overtopping the older and less vigorous growths, and stifling them by its shade.

OUR MERELY SOCIAL INTOLERANCE KILLS NO ONE, ROOTS OUT NO OPINIONS, BUT INDUCES MEN TO DISGUISE THEM, OR TO ABSTAIN FROM ANY ACTIVE EFFORT FOR THEIR DIFFUSION.

With us, heretical opinions do not perceptibly gain, or even lose, ground in each decade or generation; they never blaze out far and wide, but continue to smoulder in the narrow circles of thinking and studious persons among whom they originate, without ever lighting up the general affairs of mankind with either a true or a deceptive light. And thus is kept up a state of things very satisfactory to some minds, because, without the unpleasant process of fining or imprisoning anybody, it maintains all prevailing opinions outwardly undisturbed, while it does not absolutely interdict the exercise of reason by dissentients afflicted with the malady of thought. A convenient plan for having peace in the intellectual world, and keeping all things going on therein very much as they do already. But the price paid for this sort of intellectual pacification, is the sacrifice of the entire

moral courage of the human mind.

A state of things in which a large portion of the most active and inquiring intellects find it advisable to keep the genuine principles and grounds of their convictions within their own breasts, and attempt, in what they address to the public, to fit as much as they can of their own conclusions to premises which they have internally renounced, cannot send forth the open, fearless characters, and logical, consistent intellects who once adorned the thinking world. The sort of men who can be looked for under it, are either mere conformers to commonplace, or time-servers for truth, whose arguments on all great subjects are meant for their hearers, and are not those which have convinced themselves. Those who avoid this alternative, do so by narrowing their thoughts and interest to things which can be spoken of without venturing within the region of principles, that is, to small practical matters, which would come right of themselves, if but the minds of mankind were strengthened and enlarged, and which will never be made effectually right until then: while that which would strengthen and enlarge men's minds, free and daring speculation on the highest subjects, is abandoned.

Those in whose eyes this reticence on the part of heretics is no evil, should consider in the first place, that in consequence of it there is never any fair and thorough discussion of heretical opinions; and that such of them as could not stand such a discussion, though they may be prevented from spreading, do not disappear.

BUT IT IS NOT THE MINDS OF HERETICS THAT ARE DETERIORATED MOST, BY THE BAN PLACED ON ALL INQUIRY WHICH DOES NOT END IN THE ORTHODOX CONCLUSIONS. THE GREATEST HARM DONE IS TO THOSE WHO ARE NOT HERETICS, AND WHOSE WHOLE MENTAL DEVELOPMENT IS CRAMPED, AND THEIR REASON COWED, BY THE FEAR OF HERESY.

Who can compute what the world loses in the multitude of promising intellects combined with timid characters, who dare not follow out any bold, vigorous, independent train of thought, lest it should land them in something which would admit of being considered irreligious or immoral? Among them we may occasionally see some man of deep conscientiousness, and subtle and refined understanding, who spends a life in sophisticating with an intellect which he cannot silence, and exhausts the resources of ingenuity in attempting to reconcile the promptings of his conscience and reason with orthodoxy, which yet he does not, perhaps, to the end succeed in doing. No one can be a great thinker who does not recognise, that as a thinker it is his first duty to follow his intellect to whatever conclusions it may lead. Truth gains more even by the errors of one who, with due study and preparation, thinks for himself, than by the true opinions of those who only hold them because they do not suffer themselves to think.

Not that it is solely, or chiefly, to form great thinkers, that freedom of thinking is required. On the contrary, it is as much and even more indispensable, to enable average human beings to attain the mental stature which they are capable of. There have been, and may again be, great individual thinkers, in a general atmosphere of mental slavery. But there never has been, nor ever will be, in that atmosphere, an intellectually active people. When any people has made a temporary approach to such a character, it has been because the dread of heterodox speculation was for a time suspended. Where there is a tacit convention that principles are not to be disputed; where the discussion of the greatest questions which can occupy humanity is considered to be closed, we cannot hope to find that generally high scale of mental activity which has made some periods of history so remarkable. Never when controversy avoided the subjects which are large and important enough to kindle enthusiasm, was the mind of a people stirred up from its foundations, and the impulse given which raised even persons of the most ordinary intellect

to something of the dignity of thinking beings. Of such we have had an example in the condition of Europe during the times immediately following the Reformation; another, though limited to the Continent and to a more cultivated class, in the speculative movement of the latter half of the eighteenth century; and a third, of still briefer duration, in the intellectual fermentation of Germany during the Goethian and Fichtean period. These periods differed widely in the particular opinions which they developed; but were alike in this, that during all three the yoke of authority was broken. In each, an old mental despotism had been thrown off, and no new one had yet taken its place. The impulse given at these three periods has made Europe what it now is. Every single improvement which has taken place either in the human mind or in institutions, may be traced distinctly to one or other of them. Appearances have for some time indicated that all three impulses are well nigh spent; and we can expect no fresh start...

...until we again assert our mental freedom.

MILL'S SECOND ARGUMENT: "HE WHO KNOWS

Let us now pass to the second division of the argument, and dismissing the supposition that any of the received opinions may be false, let us assume them to be true, and examine into the worth of the manner in which they are likely to be held, when their truth is not freely and openly canvassed. However unwillingly a person who has a strong opinion may admit the possibility that his opinion may be false, he ought to be moved by the consideration that however true it may be, if it is not fully, frequently, and fearlessly discussed, it will be held as a dead dogma, not a living truth.

There is a class of persons (happily not quite so numerous as formerly) who think it enough if a person assents undoubtingly to what they think true, though he has no knowledge whatever of the grounds of the opinion, and could not make a tenable defence of it against the most superficial objections. Such persons, if they can once get their creed taught from authority, naturally think that no good, and some harm, comes of its being allowed to be questioned. Where their influence prevails, they make it nearly impossible for the received opinion to be rejected wisely and considerately, though it may still be rejected rashly and ignorantly; for to shut out discussion entirely is seldom possible, and when it once gets in, **BELIEFS NOT GROUNDED ON CONVICTION ARE APT TO GIVE WAY BEFORE THE SLIGHTEST SEMBLANCE OF AN ARGUMENT.** {...} However, this possibility—assuming that the true opinion abides in the mind, but abides as a prejudice, a belief independent of, and proof against, argument—is not the way in which truth ought to be held by a rational being. This is not knowing the truth. Truth, thus held, is but one superstition the more, accidentally clinging to the words which enunciate a truth.

{...} Whatever people believe, on subjects on which it is of the first importance to believe rightly, they ought to be able to defend against at least the common objections. But, someone may say, "Let them be taught the grounds of their opinions. It does not follow that opinions must be merely parroted because they are never heard controverted. Persons who learn geometry do not simply commit the theorems to memory, but understand and learn likewise the demonstrations; and it would be absurd to say that they remain ignorant of the grounds of geometrical truths, because they never hear any one deny, and attempt to disprove them."

Undoubtedly: and such teaching suffices on a subject like mathematics, where there is nothing at all to be said on the wrong side of the question. The peculiarity of the evidence of mathematical truths is, that all the argument is on one side. There are no objections, and no answers to objections. But on every subject on which difference of opinion is possible, the truth depends on a balance to be struck between two sets of conflicting reasons. Even in natural philosophy, there is always some other explanation possible of the same facts; some geocentric theory instead of heliocentric, some phlogiston instead of oxygen; and it has to be shown why that other theory cannot be the true one: and until this is shown, and until we know how it is shown, we do not understand the grounds of our opinion. But when we turn to subjects infinitely more complicated, to morals, religion, politics, social relations, and the business of life, three-fourths of the arguments for every disputed opinion consist in dispelling the appearances which favour some opinion different from it. The greatest orator, save one, of antiquity [Cicero], has left it on record that he always studied his adversary's case with as great, if not with still greater, intensity than even his own. What Cicero practised as the means of forensic success, requires to be imitated by all who study any subject in order to arrive at the truth.

He who knows only his own side of the

case, knows little of that. His reasons may be good, and no one may have been able to refute them. But if he is equally unable to refute the reasons on the opposite side; if he does not so much as know what they are, he has no ground for preferring either opinion. The rational position for him would be suspension of judgment, and unless he contents himself with that, he is either led by authority, or adopts, like the generality of the world, the side to which he feels most inclination.

Nor is it enough that he should hear the arguments of adversaries from his own teachers, presented as they state them, and accompanied by what they offer as refutations. That is not the way to do justice to the arguments, or bring them into real contact with his own mind. He must be able to hear them from persons who actually believe them; who defend them in earnest, and do their very utmost for them. He must know them in their most plausible and persuasive form; **HE MUST FEEL THE WHOLE FORCE OF THE DIFFICULTY WHICH THE TRUE VIEW OF THE SUBJECT HAS TO ENCOUNTER AND DISPOSE OF; ELSE HE WILL NEVER REALLY POSSESS HIMSELF OF THE PORTION OF TRUTH WHICH MEETS AND REMOVES THAT DIFFICULTY.**

Ninety-nine in a hundred of what are called educated men are in this condition; even of those who can argue fluently for their opinions. Their conclusion may be true, but it might be false for anything they know: they have never thrown themselves into the mental position of those who think differently from them, and considered what such persons may have to say; and consequently they do not, in any proper sense of the word, know the doctrine which they themselves profess. They do not know those parts of it which explain and justify the remainder; the considerations which show that a fact which seemingly conflicts with another is reconcilable with it, or that, of two apparently strong reasons, one and not the other ought to be preferred. All that part of the truth which {...} decides the judgment of a completely informed mind, they are strangers to; nor is it ever really known, but to those who have attended equally and impartially to both sides, and endeavoured to see the reasons of both in the strongest light. So essential is this discipline to a real understanding of moral and human subjects, that if opponents of all important truths do not exist, it is indispensable to imagine them, and supply them with the strongest arguments which the most skilful devil's advocate can conjure up.

To abate the force of these considerations, an enemy of free discussion may be supposed to say, that there is no necessity for mankind in general to know and understand all that can be said against or for their opinions by philosophers and theologians. That it is not needful for common men to be able to expose all the misstatements or fallacies of an ingenious opponent. That it is enough if there is always somebody capable of answering them, so that nothing likely to mislead uninstructed persons remains unrefuted. That simple minds, having been taught the obvious grounds of the truths inculcated on them, may trust to authority for the rest, and being aware that they have neither knowledge nor talent to resolve every difficulty which can be raised, may repose in the assurance that all those which have been raised have been or can be answered, by those who are specially trained to the task.

Conceding to this view of the subject the utmost that can be claimed for it by those most easily satisfied with the amount of understanding of truth which ought to accompany the belief of it; even so, the argument for free discussion is no way weakened. For even this doctrine acknowledges that mankind ought to have a rational assurance that all objections have been satisfactorily answered; and how are they to be answered if that which requires to be answered is not spoken? Or how can the answer be known to be satisfactory, if the objectors have no opportunity of showing that it is unsatisfactory? If not the public, at least the philosophers and theologians who are to resolve the difficulties, must make themselves familiar with those difficulties in their most puzzling form: and this cannot be accomplished unless they are freely stated, and placed in the most advantageous light which they admit of. {...}

If, however, the mischievous operation of the absence of free discussion, when the received opinions are true, were confined to leaving men ignorant of the grounds of those opinions, it might be thought that this, if an intellectual, is no moral evil, and does not affect the worth of the opinions, regarded in their influence on the character. The fact, however, is, that not only the grounds of the opinion are forgotten in the absence of discussion, but too often the meaning of the opinion itself. The words which convey it, cease to suggest ideas, or suggest only a small portion of those they were originally employed to communicate.

INSTEAD OF A VIVID CONCEPTION AND A LIVING BELIEF, THERE REMAIN ONLY A FEW PHRASES RETAINED BY ROTE; OR, IF ANY PART, THE SHELL AND HUSK ONLY OF THE MEANING IS RETAINED, THE FINER ESSENCE BEING LOST.
{...} It is illustrated in the experience of almost all ethical doctrines and religious creeds. They are all full of meaning and vitality to those who originate them, and

to the direct disciples of the originators. Their meaning continues to be felt in undiminished strength, and is perhaps brought out into even fuller consciousness, so long as the struggle lasts to give the doctrine or creed an ascendancy over other creeds. At last it either prevails, and becomes the general opinion, or its progress stops; it keeps possession of the ground it has gained, but ceases to spread further. When either of these results has become apparent, controversy on the subject flags, and gradually dies away. The doctrine has taken its place, if not as a received opinion, as one of the admitted sects or divisions of opinion: those who hold it have generally inherited, not adopted it; and conversion from one of these doctrines to another, being now an exceptional fact, occupies little place in the thoughts of their professors. Instead of being, as at first, constantly on the alert either to defend themselves against the world, or to bring the world over to them, they have subsided into acquiescence, and neither listen, when they can help it, to arguments against their creed, nor trouble dissentients [dissenters] (if there be such) with arguments in its favour. From this time may usually be dated the decline in the living power of the doctrine.

We often hear the teachers of all creeds lamenting the difficulty of keeping up in the minds of believers a lively apprehension of the truth which they nominally recognise, so that it may penetrate the feelings, and acquire a real mastery over the conduct. No such difficulty is complained of while the creed is still fighting for its existence; even the weaker combatants then know and feel what they are fighting for, and the difference between it and other doctrines; and in that period of every creed's existence, not a few persons may be found, who have realized its fundamental principles in all the forms of thought, have weighed and considered them in all their important bearings, and have experienced the full effect on the character, which belief in that creed ought to produce in a mind thoroughly imbued with it. But when it has come to be an hereditary creed, and to be received passively, not actively—when the mind is no longer compelled, in the same degree as at first, to exercise its vital powers on the questions which its belief presents to it, there is a progressive tendency to forget all of the belief except the formularies, or to give it a dull and torpid assent, as if accepting it on trust dispensed with the necessity of realizing it in consciousness, or testing it by personal experience; until it almost ceases to connect itself at all with the inner life of the human being. Then are seen the cases, so frequent in this age of the world as almost to form the majority, in which the creed remains as it were outside the mind, incrusting and petrifying it against all other influences addressed to the higher parts of our nature; manifesting its power by not suffering any fresh and living conviction to get in, but itself doing nothing for the mind or heart, except standing sentinel over them to keep them vacant. {...} **BOTH TEACHERS AND LEARNERS GO TO SLEEP AT THEIR POST, AS SOON AS THERE IS NO ENEMY IN THE FIELD.**

The same thing holds true, generally speaking, of all traditional doctrines—those of prudence and knowledge of life, as well as of morals or religion. All languages and literatures are full of general observations on life, both as to what it is, and how to conduct oneself in it; observations which everybody knows, which everybody repeats, or hears with acquiescence, which are received as truisms, yet of which most people first truly learn the meaning, when experience, generally of a painful kind, has made it a reality to them. How often, when smarting under some unforeseen misfortune or disappointment, does a person call to mind some proverb or common saying, familiar to him all his life, the meaning of which, if he had ever before felt it as he does now, would have saved him from the calamity. There are indeed reasons for this, other than the absence of discussion: there are many truths of which the full meaning cannot be realized, until personal experience has brought it home. But much more of the meaning even of these would have been understood, and what was understood would have been far more deeply impressed on the mind, if the man had been accustomed to hear it argued pro and con by people who did understand it. The fatal tendency of mankind to leave off thinking about a thing when it is no longer doubtful, is the cause of half their errors. **A CONTEMPORARY AUTHOR HAS WELL SPOKEN OF "THE DEEP SLUMBER OF A DECIDED OPINION."**

But {...} is the absence of unanimity an indispensable condition of true knowledge? Is it necessary that some part of mankind should persist in error, to enable any to realize the truth? Does a belief cease to be real and vital as soon as it is generally received—and is a proposition never thoroughly understood and felt unless some doubt of it remains? As soon as mankind have unanimously accepted a truth, does the truth perish within them? The highest aim and best result of improved intelligence, it has hitherto been thought, is to unite mankind more and more in the acknowledgment of all important truths: and does the intelligence only last as long as it has not achieved its object? Do the fruits of conquest perish by the very completeness of the victory?

I affirm no such thing. As mankind improve, the number of doctrines which are no longer disputed or doubted will be constantly on the increase: and the well-being of mankind may almost be measured by the number and gravity of the truths which have reached the point of being uncontested. The cessation, on one question after another, of serious controversy, is one of the necessary incidents of the consolidation of opinion; a consolidation as salutary in the case of true opinions, as it is dangerous and noxious when the opinions are erroneous. But though this gradual narrowing of the bounds of diversity of opinion is necessary in both senses of the term, being at once inevitable and indispensable, we are not therefore obliged to conclude that all its consequences must be beneficial.

The loss of so important an aid to the intelligent and living apprehension of a truth, as is afforded by the necessity of explaining it to, or defending it against, opponents, though not sufficient to outweigh, is no trifling drawback from, the benefit of its universal recognition. Where this advantage can no longer be had, I confess I should like to see the teachers of mankind endeavouring to provide a substitute for it; some contrivance for making the difficulties of the question as present to the learner's consciousness, as if they were pressed upon him by a dissentient champion, eager for his conversion.

But instead of seeking contrivances for this purpose, they have lost those they formerly had. The Socratic dialectics, so magnificently exemplified in the dialogues of Plato, were a contrivance of this description. They were essentially a negative discussion of the great questions of philosophy and life, directed with consummate skill to the purpose of convincing any one who had merely adopted the commonplaces of received opinion, that he did not understand the subject—that he as yet attached no definite meaning to the doctrines he professed; in order that, becoming aware of his ignorance, he might be put in the way to attain a stable belief, resting on a clear apprehension both of the meaning of doctrines and of their evidence. The school disputations of the middle ages had a somewhat similar object. They were intended to make sure that the pupil understood his own opinion, and (by necessary correlation) the opinion opposed to it, and could enforce the grounds of the one and confute those of the other. These last-mentioned contests had indeed the incurable defect, that the premises appealed to were taken from authority, not from reason; and, as a discipline to the mind, they were in every respect inferior to the powerful dialectics which formed the intellects of the Socratici viri [Socratic thinkers] but the modern mind owes far more to both than it is generally willing to admit. {...}

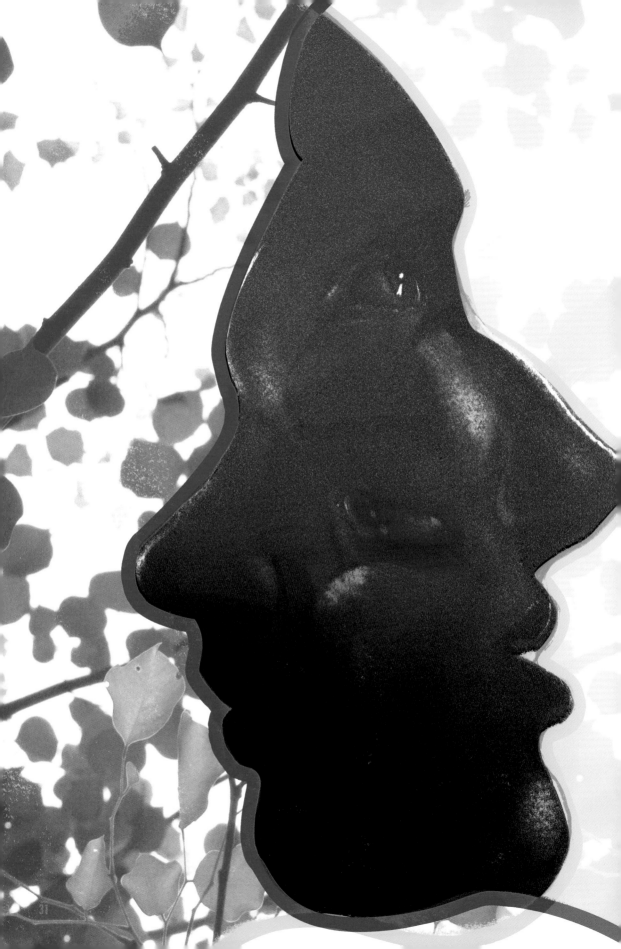

"CONFLICTING DOCTRINES SHARE THE TRUTH BETWEEN THEM"

It still remains to speak of one of the principal causes which make diversity of opinion advantageous, and will continue to do so until mankind shall have entered a stage of intellectual advancement which at present seems at an incalculable distance. We have hitherto considered only two possibilities: that the received opinion may be false, and some other opinion, consequently, true; or that, the received opinion being true, a conflict with the opposite error is essential to a clear apprehension and deep feeling of its truth. But there is a commoner case than either of these; when the conflicting doctrines, instead of being one true and the other false, share the truth between them; and the nonconforming opinion is needed to supply the remainder of the truth, of which the received doctrine embodies only a part. Popular opinions, on subjects not palpable to sense, are often true, but seldom or never the whole truth. They are a part of the truth; sometimes a greater, sometimes a smaller part, but exaggerated, distorted, and disjoined from the truths by which they ought to be accompanied and limited. Heretical opinions, on the other hand, are generally some of these suppressed and neglected truths, bursting the bonds which kept them down, and either seeking reconciliation with the truth contained in the common opinion, or fronting it as ene-mies, and setting themselves up, with similar exclusiveness, as the whole truth. The latter case is hitherto the most frequent, as, in the human mind, one-sidedness has always been the rule, and many-sidedness the exception. Hence, even in revolutions of opinion, one part of the truth usually sets while another rises.

Even progress, which ought to superadd, for the most part only substitutes, one partial and incomplete truth for another; improvement consisting chiefly in this, that the new fragment of truth is more wanted, more adapted to the needs of the time, than that which it displaces. Such being the partial character of prevailing opinions, even when resting on a true foundation, **EVERY OPINION WHICH EM-BODIES SOMEWHAT OF THE PORTION OF TRUTH WHICH THE COMMON OPINION OMITS, OUGHT TO BE CONSIDERED PRE-CIOUS, WITH WHATEVER AMOUNT OF ER-ROR AND CONFUSION THAT TRUTH MAY BE BLENDED.** No sober judge of human affairs will feel bound to be indignant because those who force on our notice truths which we should otherwise have overlooked, overlook some of those which we see. Rather, he will think that so long as popular truth is one-sided, it is more desirable than otherwise that unpopular truth should have one-sided asserters too;

such being usually the most energetic, and the most likely to compel reluctant at-tention to the fragment of wisdom which they proclaim as if it were the whole.

Thus, in the eighteenth century, when nearly all the instructed, and all those of the uninstructed who were led by them, were lost in admiration of what is called civilization, and of the marvels of modern science, literature, and philosophy, and while greatly overrating the amount of unlikeness between the men of modern and those of ancient times, indulged the belief that the whole of the difference was in their own favour; with what a salu-tary shock did the paradoxes of Rousseau explode like bombshells in the midst, dislocating the compact mass of one-sid-ed opinion, and forcing its elements to recombine in a better form and with ad-ditional ingredients. Not that the current opinions were on the whole farther from the truth than Rousseau's were; on the contrary, they were nearer to it; they con-tained more of positive truth, and very much less of error.

Nevertheless there lay in Rousseau's doc-trine, and has floated down the stream of opinion along with it, a considerable amount of exactly those truths which the popular opinion wanted; and these are the deposit which was left behind when

TRUTH

ERROR

ERROR

the flood subsided. The superior worth of simplicity of life, the enervating and demoralizing effect of the trammels and hypocrisies of artificial society, are ideas which have never been entirely absent from cultivated minds since Rousseau wrote; and they will in time produce their due effect, though at present needing to be asserted as much as ever, and to be asserted by deeds, for words, on this subject, have nearly exhausted their power...

TRUTH, IN THE GREAT PRACTICAL CONCERNS OF LIFE, IS SO MUCH A QUESTION OF THE RECONCILING AND COMBINING OF OPPOSITES, that very few have minds sufficiently capacious and impartial to make the adjustment with an approach to correctness, and it has to be made by the rough process of a struggle between combatants fighting under hostile banners… When there are persons to be found, who form an exception to the apparent unanimity of the world on any subject, even if the world is in the right, it is always probable that dissentients have something worth hearing to say for themselves, and that truth would lose something by their silence.

It may be objected, "But some received principles, especially on the highest and most vital subjects, are more than half-truths. The Christian morality, for instance, is the whole truth on that subject, and if anyone teaches a morality which varies from it, he is wholly in error."… [But] the exclusive pretension made by a part of the truth to be the whole, must and ought to be protested against; and if a reactionary impulse should make the protestors unjust in their turn, this one-sidedness, like the other, may be lamented, but must be tolerated. If Christians would teach infidels to be just to Christianity, they should themselves be just to infidelity. It can do truth no service to blink [ignore] the fact, known to all who have the most ordinary acquaintance with literary history, that a large portion of the noblest and most valuable moral teaching has been the work, not only of men who did not know, but of men who knew and rejected, the Christian faith.

I do not pretend that the most unlimited use of the freedom of enunciating all possible opinions would put an end to the evils of religious or philosophical sectarianism. Every truth which men of narrow capacity are in earnest about, is sure to be asserted, inculcated, and in many ways even acted on, as if no other truth existed in the world, or at all events none that could limit or qualify the first. I acknowledge that the tendency of all opinions to become sectarian is not cured by the freest discussion, but is often heightened and ex-

acerbated thereby; the truth which ought to have been, but was not, seen, being rejected all the more violently because proclaimed by persons regarded as opponents.

But it is not on the impassioned partisan, it is on the calmer and more disinterested bystander, that this collision of opinions works its salutary effect. **NOT THE VIOLENT CONFLICT BETWEEN PARTS OF THE TRUTH, BUT THE QUIET SUPPRESSION OF HALF OF IT, IS THE FORMIDABLE EVIL; THERE IS ALWAYS HOPE WHEN PEOPLE ARE FORCED TO LISTEN TO BOTH SIDES;** it is when they attend only to one that errors harden into prejudices, and truth itself ceases to have the effect of truth, by being exaggerated into falsehood. And since there are few mental attributes more rare than that judicial faculty which can sit in intelligent judgment between two sides of a question, of which only one is represented by an advocate before it, truth has no chance but in proportion as every side of it, every opinion which embodies

any fraction of the truth, not only finds advocates, but is so advocated as to be listened to...

Before quitting the subject of freedom of opinion, it is fit to take some notice of those who say, that the free expression of all opinions should be permitted, on condition that the manner be temperate, and do not pass the bounds of fair discussion. Much might be said on the impossibility of fixing where these supposed bounds are to be placed; for if the test be offence to those whose opinion is attacked. I think experience testifies that this offence is given whenever the attack is telling and powerful, and that every opponent who pushes them hard, and whom they find it difficult to answer, appears to them, if he shows any strong feeling on the subject, an intemperate opponent.

But this, though an important consideration in a practical point of view, merges in a more fundamental objection. Undoubtedly the manner of asserting an opinion, even though it be a true one, may be very objectionable, and may justly incur severe censure. But the principal offences of the kind are such as it is mostly impossible, unless by accidental self-betrayal, to bring home to conviction. The gravest of them is, to argue sophistically, to suppress facts or arguments, to misstate the elements of the case, or misrepresent the opposite opinion. But all this, even to the most aggravated degree, is so continually done in perfect good faith, by persons who are not considered, and in many other respects may not deserve to be considered, ignorant or incompetent, that it is rarely possible on adequate grounds conscientiously to stamp the misrepresentation as morally culpable; and still less could law presume to interfere with this kind of controversial misconduct.

With regard to what is commonly meant by intemperate discussion, namely invective, sarcasm, personality, and the like, the denunciation of these weapons would deserve more sympathy if it were ever proposed to interdict them equally to both sides; but it is only desired to restrain the employment of them against the prevailing opinion: against the unprevailing they may not only be used without general disapproval, but will be likely to obtain for him who uses them the praise of honest zeal and righteous indignation. Yet whatever mischief arises from their use, is

greatest when they are employed against the comparatively defenceless: and whatever unfair advantage can be derived by any opinion from this mode of asserting it, accrues almost exclusively to received opinions.

The worst offence of this kind which can be committed by a polemic, is to stigmatize those who hold the contrary opinion as bad and immoral men. To calumny of this sort, those who hold any unpopular opinion are peculiarly exposed, because they are in general few and uninfluential, and nobody but themselves feels much interested in seeing justice done them: but this weapon is, from the nature of the case, denied to those who attack a prevailing opinion: they can neither use it with safety to themselves, nor, if they could, would it do anything but recoil on their own cause. In general, opinions contrary to those commonly received can only obtain a hearing by studied moderation of language, and the most cautious avoidance of unnecessary offence, from which they hardly ever deviate even in a slight degree without losing ground: while unmeasured vituperation employed on the side of the prevailing opinion, really does deter people from professing contrary opinions, and from listening to those who profess them. For the interest, therefore, of truth and justice, it is far more important to restrain this employment of vituperative language than the other: and, for example, if it were necessary to choose, there would be much more need to discourage offensive attacks on infidelity, than on religion.

It is, however, obvious that law and authority have no business with restraining either, while opinion ought, in every instance, to determine its verdict by the circumstances of the individual case; condemning everyone, on whichever side of the argument he places himself, in whose mode of advocacy either want of candour, or malignity, bigotry, or intolerance of feeling manifest themselves; but not inferring these vices from the side which a person takes, though it be the contrary side of the question to our own: and giving merited honour to everyone, whatever opinion he may hold, who has calmness to see and honesty to state what his opponents and their opinions really are, exaggerating nothing to their discredit, keeping nothing back which tells or can be supposed to tell, in their favour.

THIS IS THE REAL MORALITY OF PUBLIC DISCUSSION: AND IF OFTEN VIOLATED, I AM HAPPY TO THINK THAT THERE ARE MANY CONTROVERSIALISTS WHO TO A GREAT EXTENT OBSERVE IT, AND A STILL GREATER NUMBER WHO CONSCIENTIOUSLY STRIVE TOWARDS IT.

A WORD FROM THE ARTIST

This was a challenge. My fear, all along, was that I'd take this timeless work and turn Mill into the teacher who tries too hard be cool. No one wants to see a 19th century philosopher spinning his chair around and saying "let's rap."

But as I began to pore over Richard and Jonathan's abridged version of the text, I realized the illustration process would require me to abridge it even further. I needed to distill this work down to a handful of concepts that I could bring to life as images. I needed these images to tell a story.

As I did this, I began to see how Mill's ideas merge and meld. Their relationship to each other became clearer, as did their wisdom. And my North Star emerged:

> "...However true [your belief] may be, if it is not fully, frequently, and fearlessly discussed, it will be held as a dead dogma, not a living truth."

Living truth versus dead dogma. This simple yet beautifully complex contrast gripped me. It was in this space between living truth and dead dogma that I saw a narrative unfold.

It begins in the wild, where one idea pollinates another and vines tangle together. It's messy and unmanaged, but there's a beauty in that mess—a dynamic, unmapped land rich with possibility.

As we explore, we pluck many types of fruit from their stems. Some are sweet, some bitter. But no matter what we taste, it's flavor is fully felt. Eventually, we come across a fruit that is not just sweet, but sustaining as well.

We've discovered a living truth—a young tree who's fruit fills us with clarity and purpose. Or, at least, that's what it feels like when we eat it. So we nurture the tree, as it nourishes us. We both grow stronger.

But nature, for all it's beauty, is not paradise. Bloom and rot share the same soil, and the scent of both lingers in the air. We're not alone in the woods. Venomous snakes slither at our feet when we approach the tree. Barbarians who feast on toxic beliefs circle our camp, eager to raze it to the ground.

But we live in the wild too—and are accustomed to its dangers. We see these threats clearly. We confront them head on. This truth we're keeping alive is alive in us as well, and it gives us the strength to drive the snakes deep into the ground, and the barbarians beyond the horizon.

But how do we make this victory permanent? How do we keep this now sacred tree safe forever?

We build walls around it. And the messy wilds of nature are exchanged for the curated beauty of a well kept garden. The tangled mess of vines are replaced with the pleasing order of an exhibit.

It lacks the dynamic of nature, but it's nice inside. The garden is lush, and the sweetest fruit is available to us. Besides, the gate is open and we're free to wander out into the wild. But most important, we've kept our sacred tree safe between its walls.

Or have we? Because while we may think for a moment we've built paradise, we still built it within nature. And one day a snake is found in the grass. Then a barbarian arrives at the gate. No longer familliar with their sight, we allow fear to take root in our garden.

So we lock the gate. And now the same iron bars that keep danger out also keep us in.

We build our walls higher and higher—until they are impossible to climb. But now they cast long shadows. And the very same stone that blocks the paths of snakes also blots out the sun.

Our once living truth slowly dies—its fruit withers on dead branches. The once green grounds that surround it decay into gray.

And soon all that remains of our once lush garden are the cold iron bars and bare stone walls of a prison.

———————————————————

I believe we're always somewhere between living truths and dead dogmas. I believe that's true for societies. I believe that's true for individuals. I believe that's true for each opinion we hold. We all split our time between exploring the wilds of new thought and tending to the garden of what we already believe.

But we need to remember how Mill describes truth. It's not an unbreakable object, but a living thing that sustains itself on the honest exchange of ideas. Once we begin to fear that exchange, then all encounters become indistinguishable from attacks. And we foolishly turn our gardens into prisons, where our once living truths wither into the dead dogma of a barren mind.

So my advice is this: don't be afraid. Take the time to leave your garden. Wander into the wilderness. Honor the ideas you love by making your understanding of them—not the walls that surround them—stronger.

-*Dave Cicirelli*

LEARN MORE

LEARN MORE ABOUT MILL:

Read Richard's biography, *John Stuart; Mill, Victorian Firebrand.*

LEARN MORE ABOUT HETERODOX ACADEMY:

Heterodox Academy is a non-profit alliance of professors from across the political spectrum who agree with Mill that "he who knows only his own side of the case, knows little of that." We advocate for increased viewpoint diversity in higher education. We offer tools and ideas that help universities create the vibrant cultures of debate that Mill thought were essential for the pursuit of truth.

Please visit us at: HeterodoxAcademy.org

Please also visit OpenMindPlatform.org, an interactive platform that any school or organization can use to foster mutual understanding across various kinds of differences. It is designed to extend the ideas in *All Minus One* and train people to reap the benefits of viewpoint diversity.

NOTE ON THE TEXT:

The text in this book is an edited selection from Chapter 2 of John Stuart Mill's essay

On Liberty, first published in London by Parker in 1859. The best online version of the whole essay can be found in *The Collected Works of John Stuart Mill, Volume XVIII - Essays on Politics* and *Society Part I, ed. John M. Robson (Toronto: University of Toronto Press, London: Routledge and Kegan Paul, 1977),* from which these excerpts are taken. Where Mill has used a word that is now rare or obscure, we have put in a more modern word [in brackets]. Deletions from the original text are marked thus: …. Some of Mill's original paragraphs have also been broken into shorter ones.

The full text is available online at: http://oll.libertyfund.org/ titles/ mill-the-collected- works-of-john-stuart-mill- volume-xviii-essays-on- politics-and-society-part-i-part-i

NOTE ON IMAGERY:

All images were either wholly illustrated by Dave Cicirelli or utilized assets obtained via standard license from Shutterstock, Inc and PetaPixel. Select images were inspired by the work of Jeff Owens (@MyMetalHand), Frank Quitely, Marius Sperlich (@mariussperlich) and El Lissitzky. Check them out!

ABOUT THE EDITORS

Richard V. Reeves is a Senior Fellow at the Brookings Institution, where he co-directs the Center on Children and Families. His research focuses on social mobility, inequality, and family change. Richard also teaches at the McCourt School of Public Policy at Georgetown University. Richard is the author of *Dream Hoarders* (2017), and *John Stuart Mill: Victorian Firebrand* (2007).

Jonathan Haidt is the Thomas Cooley Professor of Ethical Leadership at New York University Stern School of Business. He is a social psychologist who studies moral and political psychology. He is the author of three books: *The Happiness Hypothesis: Finding Modern Truth in Ancient Wisdom* (2006); *The Righteous Mind: Why Good People are Divided by Politics and Religion* (2012), and *The Coddling of The American Mind: How Good Intentions and Bad Ideas are Setting Up a Generation for Failure* (2018). He is a co-founder of Heterodox Academy.

Dave Cicirelli is an artist, author, and experiential creative director based out of Jersey City. As a creative director, he's known for immersive concert series headlined by the likes of T-Pain, Q-Tip, Diplo, and other two syllable luminaries. He's also known for independent artwork, such as *Fake Banksy Sells Out* and authoring the prescient and funny memoir of the early fake news era, *Fakebook: A True Story Based On Actual Lies* (2013). His latest endeavour is *Roschambeau!*—a company founded to bring new ideas to life.

We thank **Gerry Ohrstrom** for his financial support of this project, and we thank **Jeremy Willinger**, communications director of Heterodox Academy, for his many contributions at every stage.